DEEP STATE DEFECTOR III

DEEP STATE DEFECTOR III

Rahul Manchanda

To order additional copies of this book, contact:
Xlibris
1-888-795-4274
www.Xlibris.com
Orders@Xlibris.com
806856

Chapter 1

With Trump's Immigration Proposal, He Proves Again His Compassion and Strong Leadership

It's certainly not easy being a leader, let alone the leader of the United States of America, with all of its 325 million plus population, made up of tens of thousands of different enclaves, political viewpoints, religious differences, racial groups, and ethnic blocs.

It is infinitely more difficult to govern a nation such as the United States as opposed to unitary leadership powers such as China or even Russia since the U.S. Constitution theoretically gives a voice to each and every American of sane mind, coupled with the First Amendment, the power to reach the powers that be, often ending up right on the desk of the president.

So for Donald Trump to have finally reached a consensus, and heroically and mightily struck a balance by and between the most hardcore immigrant-hating right-wing groups and the most ultra-leftist open-border anarchists, is truly a herculean achievement and an accomplishment greater than any other president in modern-day American history.

No piece of legislation introduced in American enjoys 100 percent support from the American people, but the final resolution of most, if not all, outstanding immigration legal issues remaining is now not only a necessity, but is truly a National Security issue.

1

Rabid haters such as leftist house minority leader Nancy Pelosi angrily declare that Trump is a racist, making such wild-eyed and crazy statements that Donald Trump wants to "make America white again," or when U.S. Representative Luis Gutierrez calls Trump a *Nazi* or KKK leader.

Meanwhile hardcore right-wing pundits such as Ann Coulter harshly compare him to liberal left-wing hippies, terming his proposed immigration legislation as a *love fest* while others such as Mark Krikorian of the ultra-right-wing Center for Immigration Studies threaten Trump that he will be impeached before the 2020 election cycle.

But how can Trump be both?

How can one man be both a racist and a love-fest hippie?

The fact remains that Donald Trump is a tough, seasoned, and pragmatic New York City businessman, who knows how to weather the proverbial storm while still getting what he wants done.

This is exactly what the American people want and need, and this is exactly what the country needs at this moment in history.

For too long, weak and lame past presidents have made legislative and policy changes after first sticking their finger in the wind and implementing change based on who lobbied the hardest or paid the most money or who had the most power—with President Donald Trump, he always goes with what is right and correct, based on the consensus and data that's out there—with deft execution and finality.

This is not the mark of a politician but rather the mark of a pragmatic New York City businessman.

Not only has he promised to protect the humanity and safeguard the interests of more than 800,000 innocent kids who were brought to the United States by their law-breaking parents, but he also expanded this number to include up to 2 million in total who also fall within those categories.

In other words, he gave the *leftists* even MORE than what they asked for.

Then he turned around and placed a total stop-gap on wildly out of control *chain migration* and the veritable *crap-shoot* diversity visa lottery program, which have both seriously threatened to undermine the fabric of the American community and its security, giving time for the American people to assimilate and integrate themselves as Americans, newer ones and multi-generational.

This breathing period is important, as it was in ancient Rome, so that Americans no longer exist as *clumps* of haters attacking each other at their throats but rather settle in and settle down to "forge a new nation" as the Founding Fathers had previously envisioned.

And while Trump's detractors curse the *wall* that he wants to build, claiming that its construction is inherently *racist*. How does that explain the fact that the main reason for the wall is to keep out the hundred billion dollar per month drug business (heroin, cocaine, crystal meth, opioid, MDMA, ecstasy, and other narcotics) trafficking trade being funneled in through America's southern border?

Can one truly be racist against drugs?

Once again, the facts speak loudly for themselves—if anyone can get immigration reform done once and for all, it's the talented and tough New York City businessman from Queens, New York.

CHAPTER 2

America Should Not Only Be a Nation of Law but Also of Equity

There is a very common phrase used within the legal profession, that justice should be meted out pursuant to both *law and equity.*

Very few Americans understand the very large difference between these two terms, but their definitions and their corresponding effects on the American system of jurisprudence should not be dismissed.

Unlike in Europe, which has a relatively rigid form of legal jurisprudence based on the Justinian Code, usually called *civil law* and which is more based on *right and wrong*, black and white, with little to no negotiation or lee-way to determine what is legal and what is not, the American system of law like its fore bearer in British Law is common law based.

Common law is defined as judicial constructs being based on judicial interpretation of the laws passed by the legislative branch.

This of course leaves room for interpretation based on the moral codes of the modern day as well as political realities.

This concept can be criticized by some, in that judges have often been termed *activists* if they rule too heavily in one way or another, depending on their political viewpoints and value systems inherent in their own mind.

But still, however, Americans of all stripes are famous for declaring that the country is a *nation of laws*, not people.

But the law is very dry and very black and white, unforgiving of current realities within the American social fabric.

Enter the concept of *equity*, wherein this has been explained as the meting out of justice based on principles of *tit for tat*, or proper justice not necessarily covered by the black letter of the law alone.

Equity allows courts to apply justice based on *natural law* and on their discretion.

Whenever there is a disagreement as to the application of common law, equity is applied.

The concept of equity was developed to temper the strict set of rules or laws which were considered too harsh, draconian, or counterproductive when applied to certain cases and implements a body of *principles* which advocate *fairness* to follow natural law.

This concept of equity has come into play numerous times in our nation's history from the right of women and blacks to vote to the freeing of the slaves; to the creation of the federal civil rights laws; to striking down rampant and open discrimination against gays, Jews, and other protected class minorities; and even to such programs as protecting the environment or safety/health issues, which all were previously forbidden to be tampered with or whose existence was even outlawed by the current *laws of the land*.

So the point is Americans must not only be guided by the rule Of law, but also by the *concept of equity* so that they are able to always view problems within American society through the lens of ultimate justice and not only through the black letter of the sometimes myopic and limiting edicts of the rule of law.

Because simply following the rule of law will inevitably lead to cruel, harsh, unjust, stagnant, and ironically enough immoral, unethical or even illegal judicial decisions which would ultimately have a deleterious and negative overall effect on the soul of the country itself.

After all, it was entirely legal when Nazi Germany murdered 6–10 million of its own citizens during World War 2 when Soviet Russia murdered more than 100 million of its own people during the communist expansion and other countless and horrendous blights on human history.

To that end, America should never lose sight of, or forget, that we are not only a nation of laws but that we should also strive to be a nation of equity.

Chapter 3

Donald Trump's Domestic Policy Is America-First, but His Foreign Policy Reflects His Servitude to Deep-State, Global Oligarchs

President Donald Trump was elected by the American people in order to pursue policies designed to strengthen and fortify America's economy, position in the world, and to restore policies to protect and assist the American worker.

More specifically, Trump was elected to help protect and safeguard the American people.

But Trump's inexperience with foreign policy threatens to undermine all of this and undo all of the progress that he is making.

By placing into power Mike Pompeo as State Department chief, Gina Haspel as CIA director, and John Bolton as National Security advisor, Trump is moving the United States closer and closer to outright war, culminating in World War 3.

Obviously, China and Russia will never back down over their support of both Iran and Syria, and the Joint Comprehensive Plan of Action (JCPOA) Iran nuclear deal shelved any hope or ambition of nuclear proliferation in that country, as well as opened up that nation to full transparency inspections and monitoring by the international community, including by the USA.

And diplomacy and calmer heads have allowed North Korea to also come to the negotiating table in the last few weeks to try and place their nuclear arsenal into the dustbin of history.

But the track records of the above three individuals show that they have no interest in diplomacy or cooperative foreign policy, but rather they have focused on bullying, browbeating, chest thumping, fiery rhetoric, and provocative actions which will only bolster and fortify China and Russia's burgeoning military and economic relationship (they were strategic competitors/enemies before the neoconservatives pushed them together with their misguided foreign policy objectives, support of clandestine terrorism, ISIS, and other catastrophic decisions by the neocon foreign policy establishment led by men like John Bolton, Richard Perle, Frank Gaffney, Bill Kristol, and others).

This has also further pushed the Eurasian nations further into the orbit and influence of Russia and China while fleeing the West.

The fact remains that the United States can become great again when it comes to domestic policy even with such internationally consequential acts such as tariffs, but it can never become the preeminent international power that it used to be even ten years ago.

China and Russia have completely altered the global landscape both militarily and economically and will not budge or yield one inch in either without a major military confrontation where everyone in the world would die.

America needs to accept this reality, have some humility, cooperate with other powerful nations, and stop trying to revert back to the unipolar world order of yesterday, briefly enjoyed for a few years after the fall of the Soviet Union.

It's okay to *make America great again*, but it is both shortsighted and foolhardy to try and make the world American again without first accepting that the entire world and its people would be obliterated in the process.

CHAPTER 4

The New Global Triumvirate: Trump, Putin, and Jinping

In ancient Rome, which was the new world global order of that epoch, a new form of governance emerged—that of the triumvirate—a nonofficial, three-member council of strong leaders who brought order and prosperity to their universe.

In the late republic, two three-man political alliances are called triumvirates by modern scholars though only for the second was the term triumviri used at the time to evoke constitutional precedents.

The first triumvirate was an informal political alliance of Julius Caesar, Pompeius Magnus, and Marcus Crassus.

Even though the arrangement had no legal status, its purpose was to consolidate the political power of the three and their supporters against the senatorial elite (owned and paid for by the global deep-state oligarchs of that time period).

The second triumvirate was officially recognized as a triumvirate at that time within the purview of the *Lex Titia* which legally formalized the rule of Octavian, Mark Antony, and Marcus Aemilius Lepidus in 43 BCE.

These three-man commissions were expressly formed in order to restore the Constitution of the republic and resistance to the wealthy, powerful, deep-state corrupting forces of their day.

These triumvirates were forged during a time when the deep-state global oligarchs had thoroughly corrupted and polluted the body politic—and where the governed people were all but left out of the prosperity, wealth, and human rights enjoyed by their ruling deep-state elites.

The most important aspect of these triumvirates was the commitment by these strong leaders of their people to stand together against the bloated wealth, corruption, and domination by the deep-state oligarchs against their own people.

There is no better comparison to what the world is currently witnessing in the forms of American President Donald Trump, Chinese president Xi Jinping, and Russian president Vladimir Putin.

All three individuals rose to power hoisted up by their own hard work and tenacity, and all three never forgot or lost sight of their obligations to their own people.

Each of these men have emerged as true leaders forged from hard knocks and iron will, and they have remained true to their people while combating corruption, sloth, gluttony, waste, and discordance in their own way and in their own capacity through their own forms of national governance.

The global deep-state oligarchy of today's modern age of course wish to prevent a smooth, sinuous relationship by and between these three global leaders, who represent the most powerful, wealthy, and militarily strong nations in the world for their own selfish, avaricious, and greedy purposes. Even though if the three leaders united hands and worked together on international trade, peace, prosperity, security, and cooperation, the entire world's people would finally know peace and prosperity.

But the reality is that the deep-state oligarchs make their money and grow their own power by profiting off from war, disaster, terrorism, cacophony, chaos, addiction, distrust, corruption, false flags, fear, and the abrogation of human and civil rights.

This is why it is very important that these three global leaders resist the weapons, tools, and manipulations of the deep-state global oligarchs and their agents within the mainstream media, intelligence agencies, and international business and lock their hands together and fight united for their own people in conjunction with each other to increase trade, security, peace, universal human rights, prosperity, cooperation, and partnership throughout the world.

Each of these three world leaders have suffered incredible adversity, defeated odds, persevered, fallen, recovered, and through it all have persisted in trying to deliver for their own people, and this is the mark of a true world-class leader.

Their courage knows no bounds, and they rightfully deserve to be considered the new triumvirate of the global community.

CHAPTER 5

Whatever Happened to Due Process in International Relations?

It seems that recent events across the globe have further revealed a glaring hole within the framework and structure of international relations, law, and diplomacy—the complete and total lack of due process.

In each and every country around the world, from the local level all the way to the federal, there exists in criminal and civil jurisprudence the concept of due process—a concept which has been defined as the legal requirement that the state must respect all legal rights that are owed to a person.

Due process balances the power of law of the land and protects the individual person from it.

When a government harms a person without following the exact course of the law, this constitutes a due process violation, which offends the rule of law.

Due process has also been frequently interpreted as limiting laws and legal proceedings so that judges, instead of legislators, may define and guarantee fundamental fairness, justice, and liberty.

Analogous to the concepts of natural justice and procedural justice used in various other jurisdictions, the interpretation of due process is sometimes expressed as a command that the government must not be unfair to the people or abuse them physically.

Due process developed from clause 39 of Magna Carta in England.

Reference to due process first appeared in a statutory rendition of clause 39 in AD 1354: "No man of what state or condition he be, shall be put out of his lands or tenements nor taken, nor disinherited, nor put to death, without he be brought to answer by due process of law."

When English and American law gradually diverged, due process was not upheld in England but became incorporated in the U.S. Constitution.

While there is no definitive list of the *required procedures* that due process requires, Judge Henry Friendly (July 3, 1903 to March 11, 1986), a prominent judge in the United States, who sat on the United States Court of Appeals for the second circuit from 1959–1974, generated a list that remains highly influential, as to both content and relative priority:

(1)   An unbiased tribunal;

(2)   Notice of the proposed action and the grounds asserted for it;

(3)   Opportunity to present reasons why the proposed action should not be taken;

(4)   The right to present evidence, including the right to call witnesses;

(5)   The right to know opposing evidence;

(6)   The right to cross-examine adverse witnesses;

(7)   A decision based exclusively on the evidence presented;

(8)   Opportunity to be represented by counsel;

(9)   Requirement that the tribunal prepare a record of the evidence presented; and

(10) Requirement that the tribunal prepare written findings of fact and reasons for its decision.

The international news media, on behalf of various governmental agencies, intelligence organizations, private deep-state oligarch-run businesses has been blasting from time to time, allegations and accusations leveled by one country or empire versus another, most notably by the Western NATO powers against the Eurasian ones, that of Russia, Syria, Iran, North Korea, China, and others while the converse has not occurred at all.

This should tell us something.

Lately, the Skripal poisoning attempts, the multiple alleged Bashar Assad Syrian government chemical weapons attacks, and countless others have dominated the headlines.

Russia has been screaming from the rooftops that their greatest concern is that the USA or the West will manufacture some type of false flag attack to blame it on them.

The only solution then is that both the United Nations and the International Criminal Court must be given the power, funding, and support by countries that are being victimized by false flag allegations to be empowered to put a stop to these irresponsible lobbyings and accusations of criminal conduct by one set of nations versus the others.

When due process is absent from our nations' courts, police departments, law enforcement agencies, then innocent people get thrown into jail in criminal cases or bankrupted in civil matters.

But when nations are not afforded due process in the course of international relations, terrorism breaks out and so does the possibility of nuclear annihilation of all the worlds' people.

Chapter 6

The Deep-State, Luciferian Communist's Vested Interest in Destroying Relationships

It is no secret that healthy, stable relationships between human beings (family, friendships, others) ultimately yield a stronger, independent, balanced, and self-sufficient individual.

Countless scientific and sociological studies over hundreds of years have proved this.

So why are so many trillions of dollars being spent by the elites to fund governmental programs, technology, and societal developments to go against this and to undermine relationships within global society (especially the modern first world ones)?

The answer is quite simple—the more fragmented, isolated, and unstable relationships are between human beings, the more they can be easily controlled, first on the individual level, and then on the mass level.

The destruction of relationships by and between men and women have been the first order of business by the deep-state communists.

This is designed ultimately to constructively *orphan* young children in modern-day society to make them more pliable and vulnerable to social engineering by the elites.

As a secondary goal this is also designed to make women (and men) dependent upon the state and the deep-state Communist oligarchs who run it, also for better control and regulation of the masses.

Some of the well-funded, well-organized, and concerted efforts toward the destruction of relationships and the family unit that have literally exploded over the past few decades in the modern world, trickling down to the less well developed parts of the world, are as follows:

(1) social media and dating applications, which encourage promiscuity, cheating, lying, obfuscation, distrust, disease, and disloyalty by and between men and women, wherein some of these social media apps even proudly display their goals such as in Ashley Madison, whereby cheating and *affairs* are literally encouraged and wherein other apps like Tinder encourage quick, midday sex romps while either of the two spouses or partners in a relationship can exchange sex and bodily fluids during their thirty-minute breaks while at work or at home;

(2) the massive infusion of opioids and drugs and narcotics into everyday daily life, thus obscuring and distracting men and women from the most important pressing matters in their lives, such as their own children and family integrity;

(3) the open embrace and encouragement of third-wave feminism, which seeks to vilify and chastise healthy male-female relationships by convincing women that traditionally positive and healthy male behavior traits such as chivalry, decisiveness, character, confidence, personal and emotional strength, stability, and stoicism are now in fact oppressive, abusive, domineering, controlling, or otherwise restrictive over female freedom—these poisonous seeds usually result in female betrayal of their husbands or male relations with studies showing that the vast majority of those women usually end up in a far worse place than they were before within that relationship (poverty, divorce, welfare programs, drug abuse and addiction, social isolation, disease, real abusive relationship situations, and other tar-pits of society, usually dragging their young children in to the hell that they have created for themselves with this *liberation*);

(4)   breakdown and rejection of religion or church in modern-day society, institutions which have encapsulated wisdom over the millennia and since the early dawn of humanity, characterized and contained within the stories, myth, parables, and other life lessons in easy-to-digest and understandable bite-sized chunks of common sense and conventional wisdom, which has been replaced by progressive, Luciferian thought penned and pushed by the deep-state communist, oligarch elite;

(5)   communist governmental, social engineering programs which have legislated and encouraged the breakdown of relationships and the family unit, such as the extreme ease in securing child support and welfare programs, ease of procuring abortions and prophylactics, sexually transmitted disease treatment and diagnosis, the Violence Against Women Act (which criminalizes normal male/female relationships as *abuse* even when there is no evidence of physical or verbal abuse), "see something say something" STASI-like legislation which encourages people in relationships to seek out and report their partners for any type of independent thought or behavior which goes against the agenda of the deep-state, communist, Oligarch, Luciferian elites.

Of course, the breakdown of relationships and families ultimately leads to the breakdown of communities and cities, as well as states and eventually the country—borders and nations are a thorn in the side of the deep-state globalists, and any leader within nations that openly encourages relationships and family are immediately vilified as "nationalists, protectionists, racists, backwards, extremists," or other horrible appellations.

It is high time that the world's leaders become cognizant of these overall threats to their nation-states, communities, societies, and families and start to work together to combat these societal ills in order to preserve and grow their communities in a healthy manner because if they don't, a Luciferian slave-master, global dictatorship is right around the corner, and the inertia will just be too great to overcome and reverse if it has not become so already.

———

CHAPTER 7

Tax Fraud Allegations Are a Mechanism of Deep-State Communist Control

When the U.S. income tax law passed in 1913 like a thief in the night, literally, when 90 percent of the U.S. Congress and Senate were home for the Christmas holidays; few people in America knew exactly what this meant.

As part of the Federal Reserve Act, which brought us our sprawling Central Bank that many early U.S. presidents such as Andrew Jackson fought against, including wars, the Sixteenth Amendment to the U.S. Constitution was ratified in 1913.

It states: "The Congress shall have power to lay and collect taxes on incomes, from whatever source derived, without apportionment among the several States, and without regard to any census or enumeration."

A few decades prior around 1894, the income tax was in fact declared unconstitutional by Article I, Section 9 of the U.S. Constitution which states: "No Capitation, or other direct, Tax shall be laid, unless in Proportion to the Census or enumeration herein before directed to be taken."

In 1894, congress passed the Wilson-Gorman Tariff, which created an income tax of 2 percent on income of over $4,000.

Charles Pollock contested that the tax was unconstitutional under Article 1, Section 9.

As such, the Supreme Court granted *certiorari* to hear this issue in *Pollock v. Farmers' Loan and Trust Company*, 157 US 429 (1895).

In Pollock, the court held that the Wilson-Gorman Tariff was unconstitutional under Article I, Section 9 of the Constitution, as the act created a direct taxation on property owners, not a tax apportioned among the states.

But all of this was in fact nullified by the above described 1913 ratification of the 16th Amendment.

Flash forward and throughout history we have seen various members of the U.S. government go after men like Al Capone for tax evasion/tax fraud when they couldn't convict their chosen and proverbial *enemy of the state* on any obvious crimes.

But no one in America really complained because everyone knew that Al Capone was a criminal, mob gangster directly responsible for countless murders, death, misery, drugs/alcohol, vice, prostitution, and other such social ills.

And so the American people let this ride for decades without raising an eyebrow.

Now, however, if one reads the mainstream news, men like Paul Manafort and Michael Cohen, people who were close to U.S. President Donald Trump, are falling to rogue U.S. attorneys and their politically motivated crusades sounding in *tax evasion* or *tax fraud* and other such nonsense.

If these men, one a highly sophisticated attorney in New York City, the other a gifted international political lobbyist who used to work for such men as President Ronald Reagan or Senator Bob Dole, can fall prey to convictions or plea agreements based on the enormously complicated and convoluted IRS Tax Code and its myriad landmines contained therein, then how about the rest of the approximately 300 million American citizens that do not even have 1/100 of the knowledge, tax professionals, accountants, record keepers, or knowledge of the law that these two men had?

The answer is quite obvious—tax evasion/tax fraud allegations are inherently biased and politicized to go after the enemies of the day, by the powers that be.

Quite simply, one must remember the phrase cui bono or "who benefits?"

The enemies of President Donald Trump within the US deep state, in their bloodthirsty quest for communist control, the United States of America (and the rest of the world) are completely and totally behind this.

And who runs the US deep state?

The international bankers are those who brought to the USA the 1913 income tax and the Federal Reserve and who also funded communism in the former Soviet Union.

Money and taxes are a form of control exercised by the global money masters; just as sanctions against sovereign nations are used to bring their geopolitical enemies to their knees.

Now these arrogant global bankers are turning their sights on our own American president and his inner circle, and the results are startlingly effective.

The American people need to be aware of and cognizant of this, and they must defend their chosen president from these communist, deep-state, global-banker-funded lunatics.

CHAPTER 8

The Slow Communist Subversion of the United States Has Culminated in the Brett Kavanaugh Case

What most Americans don't realize is that organized communist subversion often takes many years, if not decades, to slowly transform and convert the existing forms of their targeted government.

In this case because of its economic superiority and military powerhouse, the United States of America was always the ultimate prize or crown jewel of organized communism's objectives.

The problem of course was that *pesky* U.S. Constitution, with all of its attendant bills of rights, amendments guaranteeing such concepts as individual freedom, the presumption of innocence, the right to face one's accusers, the right to freedom of speech and expression, to bear arms, and other such inherently anti-communist/anti-monarchy protections.

To be sure, the Founding Fathers had written and drafted the constitution precisely because they wanted to throw off the yoke of tyrannical England and its draconian and oppressive king.

To that end the Founding Fathers labored intensely to put in writing a document that would guarantee all of the citizenry the rights to life, liberty, and the pursuit of happiness—the United States Constitution.

But the communists are very well familiar with the *boiling-frog* approach to communist conversion/subversion, and they have all the patience in the world because it is a disease that tends to be multi-generational, with one generation of communists imbuing and infecting another younger generation, using highly emotional issues to recruit them into their fold.

This is also known as *salami tactics*, which is a *divide-and-conquer* process of threats and alliances used to overcome opposition.

With it an aggressor can influence and eventually dominate a landscape, typically political, piece by piece.

In this fashion, the opposition is eliminated *slice by slice* until one realizes (too late) that it is gone in its entirety.

In some cases it includes the creation of several factions within the opposing political party and then dismantling that party from the inside without causing the *sliced* sides to protest.

Salami tactics are most likely to succeed when the perpetrators keep their true long-term motives hidden and maintain a posture of cooperativeness and helpfulness while engaged in the intended gradual subversion.

These *emotional issues* were cleverly elucidated and crystalized to be usually one of the following *special protected classes*—minority (mainly African-American) rights, gay rights, Jewish (Zionist) rights against perceived antisemitism, and finally female rights known in its extreme form as *militant feminism.*

To be sure, none of the controllers or handlers of modern-day communism give a damn about any of these four basic special-protected classes, or their rights, as they as a rule consist mainly of Luciferian, atheistic, oligarch types who are at odds with human and civil rights and instead wish to control, cull, and enslave the masses of the global population, using any and all means necessary.

When it comes to the militant feminist movement, what these global communists have succeeded in doing, over the past few decades, is *moving the goal post* even farther and farther to the left, overtly criminalizing basic male-female sexual behavior to the point of insanity.

Thus if one were to watch popular movies, read popular literature, or even speak to older generations of people, what was once considered *normal sexual behavior* by and between men and women has now become overtly criminal in nature.

The global communists have challenged human nature and wish to assert their dominion over all things, including basic fundamental human nature.

These communists have designated themselves as god, as is the essence of true pure Luciferianism.

In true *boiling-frog* methodology, they have spent the last few decades, since the feminist movement and fast forwarded in the wake of the passage of the 1994 Violence Against Women's Act (VAWA) by communist tools Joseph Biden and Bill Clinton to go after and prosecute aggressively at first, unknown or minority targets, because that way most white mainstream Americans wouldn't care or wouldn't notice.

In truly inverted and twisted logic, these global communists used what happened to them in Europe as targets against the rest of the healthy world populace who were against them—by quoting Martin Niemöller, the noted German religious scholar, when he said: *"In Germany they came first for the Communists, and I didn't speak up because I wasn't a Communist. Then they came for the Jews, and I didn't speak up because I wasn't a Jew. Then they came for the trade unionists, and I didn't speak up because I wasn't a trade unionist. Then they came for the Catholics, and I didn't speak up because I was a Protestant. Then they came for me, and by that time no one was left to speak up for me."*

This methodology also worked in the wake of September 11 when the DHS and TSA went after mainly Muslim young men between the ages of 17-35, and since no one protested or cared, now it has applied to all, including white Christian grandmothers and even babies.

Getting back to the above, first these communists, using the VAWA laws and feminist movement, began targeting, incarcerating, setting up, fining, destroying the relationships, and even murdering poor, uneducated, minority, and other *invisible* classes of society in America in order to accomplish the following goals: (1) get certain government officials in the judiciary, legislature, and executive branch to out and open themselves as those who were *willing to play the game* and help to implement their communist manifesto; (2) get case law, history, and culture to shift slowly over decades and time so that this kind of targeting became the culturally accepted norm; and (3) weed all of those out of government/power who would obstruct their vision and actually fight for and enforce the civil liberties and human rights enshrined in the Constitution and fundamental natural human behavior.

This patient *waiting game* has now yielded fruit, and in their last ditches of cynical openness about their agenda right before they launched a massive attack and onslaught against supreme court justice nominee Brett Kavanaugh, they nailed to the wall Bill Cosby, with total impunity, because as they cynically (and correctly) believed (and which may be true) that White America still consistently does not care about African-American or black America and will still allow the latter to go through any type of torture without them ever saying anything or protecting them.

This is another reason that global communists justify their beliefs—that the people are essentially *animals* anyway, who don't even care for another, so why should they care about them?

But their ultimate target is Brett Kavanaugh because he alone, as a high-level judge on the highest court in the land, would be the only one who could both undo and reverse the decades-long communism subversion of the United States, using their best tool in their toolbox—organized third-wave feminism, which has proven to be far more successful in upending and turning over the very foundations of the United States by dividing and turning against one another, men and women in their own homes.

Brett Kavanaugh, along with fellow U.S. Supreme Court Justice Neil Gorsuch, would immediately begin to beat back organized communism in the form of organized militant feminism and begin to liberate America from their yoke of tyranny and oppression.

They would restore the basic truths and rights enunciated in the US Constitution, and this of course, the organized global communists could never abide by.

This is why he is their ultimate threat and consequently their ultimate target.

It is up to every patriotic American to both recognize this and ensure that these organized global communists do not win in denying Judge Brett Kavanaugh a seat on the United State Supreme Court.

CHAPTER 9

How the New York City Communist/ Leftist Government Deals with Prominent Conservatives/ Republicans and Whistleblowers

To be a conservative or Republican within the city limits of New York City is an abject nightmare—to be a prominent one with outspoken views on preserving the United States Constitution, supporting smaller government, encouraging fiscal responsibility, maintaining a strong stance against institutionalized corruption and deeply embedded socialism within the countless governmental agencies that seek to regulate each and every aspect of one's life is a virtual death sentence.

When one or more members of the ultra-left-wing communist infiltrated New York City government (remember the en masse immigration of tens of thousands of card carrying communists and Nazis after World War 2 into the Upper West Side of Manhattan during Operation Paperclip, who thoroughly infiltrated and set out to control the machinery of the local New York City government—all five boroughs) identify a conservative, Republican, who is both prominent and has the potential to run for political office (see Michael Grimm, Dinesh D'Souza, Donald Trump for example), they immediately set in motion the various tactics and skills that they have achieved from their predecessors' establishment and work with the former Soviet Union KGB or the East German STASI with accelerated and targeted gang-stalking or *Zersetzung*, whereby they slowly, secretly, painstakingly, and relentlessly try and destroy, decompose, disorient, destabilize, and ruin their target's life, business, and family.

This imported anti-American *mafia*, with their billions upon billions of dollars in expendable cash (often stolen from Europe and the US), utilize their enormous resources within the local New York City government from bought and paid-off police officers, detectives, special agents within the New York City FBI Field Office and their selected leadership, corrupted judges in both the state and federal courts, *guns for hire* within the New York City (and state) legislature (senate and congress), various members of the countless socialist *administrative agencies*, such as those falling under the vast umbrella of the *New York City Department of Social Services* to set up, frame, entrap, and sabotage those targeted prominent conservative Republicans, ignoring their cries when they complain of crime but then backing up their tormentors with governmental immunity, coaching, funding, augmentation, and support in order to eventually and ultimately destroy their targets.

Police officers routinely ignore the complaints filed by the targets when they are victims of crime and instead coach and send the criminal back to the target this time with legal ammunition and training to go back and finish the job; judges routinely deny and cover up lawsuits and complaints filed by the targets to achieve justice. Various corrupted members of the socialist/communist governmental infrastructure open up frivolous and baseless *investigations* in order to commence unlawful surveillance, spying, espionage, wiretapping, and black-bag operations in order to gather any type of *evidence* to convict that target of a crime, all the while the New York Field Office of the FBI, instead of using the outlawed COINTELPRO gang-stalking program, uses instead the newly enacted Community Oriented Policing (COPS) program enacted by then Senator Joseph Biden and then president Bill Clinton in 1994 under the U.S. Department of Justice, currently headed by arch-criminal Rod Rosenstein, who is more akin to a secret police chief like Lavrenty Beria, Felix Dzerzhinsky, or a mob boss like Meyer Lansky.

This man Rod Rosenstein presides over the greatest criminal conspiracy ever, that is, the ultimate authority to decide on which Americans get targeted and destroyed with impunity and which ones walk in peace to prevail another day.

Unfortunately Rod Rosenstein is backed up and protected by his boss, Michael Horowitz, who is head of the Washington DC office of the Inspector General, supposedly charged with investigating the crimes of various members of the U.S. Department of Justice, Federal Bureau of Investigation, and all of the other well-funded *law enforcement* organizations throughout the United States.

To be sure, this model of clandestine communist governmental administration, totally unconstitutional and illegal sub-government within the U.S. government, is repeated throughout several major cities within the United States, such as Los Angeles, Chicago, Washington DC, Miami Florida, and other areas but none so prominent and open and strong as the one located in New York City.

The target's life is ruined and reputation sullied further by a totally compliant local media *in bed* with these conspirators, and he becomes blackballed and railroaded into suicide, death, murder, incarceration, or a mental institution should he become aware of what is happening to him.

The first step in ending this secret communist government within a constitutional United States government is first by recognizing the problem, shedding light on it, and exposing it to all Americans (and the world), all over the United States, who could then call upon their elected leaders and judges and law enforcement to challenge it head on, eradicate it, and jail those responsible, once and for all.

CHAPTER 10

American (and Global) Oligarchy Rapidly Moving toward Monarchy

Many people do not realize that the proverbial *noose* of civil rights, civil liberties, and property rights are rapidly coming to an end, in large part because of the unholy alliance by and between government and the global oligarchs (international banks and major corporations).

For example, people don't realize that current U.S. federal law permits all banks and credit unions (such as Chase Bank owned by CEO Jamie Dimon) to close any account, at any time, and for any reason, even when their own employees commit fraud, make mistakes, commit unethical acts, or otherwise screw the banking customer over for personal or political reasons, and that customer then files a legitimate complaint.

The financial institution is not required to divulge the reason(s) for account closure to the customer.

Now, when a business account is closed by a bank, the bank can (and will) retain the funds in the account for 90–180 days in order for checks, debits, chargebacks, etc., to post to the business account before the bank will mail the business customer the remaining proceeds from the account.

However, the account holder is of course not allowed access to their own hard-earned funds at all.

What this means is that these banks and credit unions have been given a universal right to steal any and all monies placed within their coffers by anyone at all, which can then be *confiscated* for any reason.

It is even so absurd that these banks and credit unions, even after they have seized or stolen your money/property, do not even have to give you a reason and can then ban you for life from ever getting your money/property back.

This same reasoning applies to nearly all of the major businesses and corporations, wherein due process has gone the way of the extinct *dodo bird*.

This is what it means when an administration (in this case Republican) talks about *bank deregulation*.

In many ways, Democrats had the right idea over Republicans when they created and enacted such banking regulatory agencies such as the Consumer Financial Protection Bureau (CFPB), recently gutted and decapitated by the Trump administration and his coterie of bought and paid for Republican conservatives.

The problem is that the same global oligarchs and international banking cartels that controlled the Democrats and enacted even more stifling Communist-type regulation to further control, cull, and choke off the American (and global) population (think Obama's Operation Chokepoint) simply use Republican deregulation as another mechanism to screw over, steal from, and rob the working and middle class by allowing these international banking cartels, credit unions, and corporations to completely do whatever they want to anyone for any reason in the absence of any regulation.

Herein lies the rub, and there has to be a middle ground, but only if the American people (and their global population counterparts) push back and vociferously tell their elected leaders to take legal and equitable action against these global thieves and criminals.

CHAPTER 11

Has the Trump Administration Lost All Compassion within Its Immigration System?

To be sure, if there was any major reason to support the Donald Trump presidential administration, one of the chief reasons would be that he is a successful New York City and international businessman, having amassed billions and billions of dollars as a savvy, intelligent, compassionate and creative man who has employed tens of thousands of workers and created a huge fortune and dynasty, building various lucrative projects and real estate ventures all over the world.

But the problem may not be with the president or his understandable policies against rampant and uncontrolled illegal immigration or the continued presence of criminal illegal aliens in the United States, but rather with the men and women that he has placed into powerful positions to run the United States Citizenship and Immigration Service (USCIS), Department of Homeland Security (DHS), Executive Office for Immigration Review (EOIR), Board of Immigration Appeals (BIA), Immigration and Customs Enforcement (ICE), Customs and Border Protection (CBP) thereon, and even further with the underlings who have been appointed under those individuals.

Many immigration lawyers, practitioners, and immigrants themselves have reported a massive uptick in seemingly dishonest behavior and underhanded tactics within the U.S. Immigration System all across the country, wherein immigrants applying under various immigration categories are being summarily denied, delayed, obstructed, cheated, or otherwise rejected for work authorization (Employment Authorization Documents or EAD) when they would normally, in the past few decades under previous administrations, be granted these automatically when their underlying applications filed at the same time (concurrently) would provide for these EADs right away even without the need for filing fees.

To be certain, these affected immigrants are not the horrific types of immigrants being paraded about in the conservative media and press, such as gang members, criminal illegal aliens, or other non-sympathetic illegal aliens, but rather these affected immigrants are people that fall into sympathetic categories such as domestic violence survivors under the Violence Against Women Act (VAWA), victims of crime under the U visa category, victims of human trafficking with T visa applicants, political asylum/refugee applicants with cases pending six months or more, and even people marrying U.S. citizens under the (c)(9) immediate visa priority date category.

Many immigration lawyers and practitioners, as well as their clients, have reported a massive increase in certain bizarre new *tactics* being used by the USCIS and their workers against people that would normally receive a work authorization card immediately upon filing.

Dishonest, illegal, and unethical tactics being used by the USCIS and its employees include such behavior such as (1) taking up many months before issuing arbitrary denials and decisions, (2) taking and cashing their filing fee checks and then rejecting their applications for strange arbitrary reasons, (3) demanding filing fee checks when none are required, (4) advising applicants to mail them back into the different incorrect addresses, (5) splitting up concurrently filed petitions so that the work authorization application portion is refused and rejected first and then turning to the underlying visa application giving them the right to work authorization getting accepted and stamped with a "receipt date notice," (6) confusing cross-mailed notices designed to create rifts and conflicts by and between immigrants and their lawyers/practitioners to destroy and sow distrust in the attorney-client relationship hoping that the immigrant will simply *give up* or *go bankrupt* and then *self deport*, (7) losing files altogether, and (8) other truly bizarre acts.

Unfortunately, this causes these immigrants (vast majority who have never been arrested or have no criminal record whatsoever) *to be forced to become criminals* in that they must find new ways to survive and thus work illegally without a lawful and bona fide work authorization card, creating a whole new class of *criminal immigrants* in order to feed themselves and their families, and then they become *ripe* to be arrested, prosecuted, deported, and have their families split up by vulture-like and ravenous Immigration Customs Enforcement (ICE) agents who seem to literally be waiting at their doors or at the companies that dared to hire them in the first place.

This practice by the USCIS also seems to be literally "cutting off the government's nose to spite its own face" by denying massive amounts of tax dollars (hundreds of billions) that would be raised by the U.S. government when these people are allowed to work legally, and thus pay their fair share of much needed taxes and revenue needed by the government— the employers would pay as these taxes are automatically deducted and calculated by the government if the immigrant worker has a legal work permit and has a social security number so even unscrupulous employers would find it difficult to dodge income and other types of employee taxes.

Even the immigration courts and the Board of Immigration Appeals (BIA) are not immune from some of these dirty, underhanded tactics, sometimes sending confusing notices and letters designed to throw the immigrant and their lawyers/representatives into disarray by inconsistently denying and then accepting jurisdiction, rejecting properly filed motions and pleadings and filings repeatedly for various ridiculous reasons, delaying and obstructing case progress and litigation, splitting up remedies for relief and purposefully obfuscating case conclusion, employing mean-spirited, incompetent, and nasty court, clerk, and DHS counsel personnel to scare or intimidate immigrants and their representatives and other behavior patterns designed to harm immigrants—and all of this has nothing to do with former U.S. Attorney General Jeff Sessions imprudently and possibly illegally took the power away from immigration judges to *close* or *terminate* immigration deportation proceedings when it would be unreasonably futile, expensive, disruptive, or frankly idiotic to continue to try and deport immigrants who have solid legal remedies and reasons to remain within the United States.

The above described troubling issues don't even address the splitting up of families at the border, but that has also been apparently going on for many years, predating the Trump Administration.

If anything, Trump's presidency has addressed this issue by trying to reunite broken-up families one by one, but this is by no means an easy or cost-effective feat, and the results of such a policy for many decades has wreaked untold havoc, hardship, pain, suffering, and trauma that no one administration could ever hope to fix—truly a human rights blemish on the United States of America for generations to come as these broken-up families, traumatized children and their offspring, and even sympathetic Americans will never forget that this had occurred on U.S. soil.

So to that end, the U.S. government, and especially its immigration service, needs to do a much better job of tackling these humanitarian issues, lest the country lose sight of the fact that it was a nation built by people leaving other countries to become immigrants run by immigrants and allowed to prosper by its immigrants.

CHAPTER 12

To Avoid War and Conflict, Iran Must Allow More Human Rights Organizations into Their Country

Upon closer inspection, it appears that the Islamic Republic of Iran has a relative near dearth of human rights organizations operating freely within that country.

Although Iran has apparently allowed the International Atomic Energy Agency and the United Nations, as all as some foreign nations to inspect from time to time its weapons facilities and nuclear power apparati, there does not seem to be a corresponding level of interest generated both externally or internally in investigating the various human rights complaints and abuses within Iran.

To be sure, this is the ultimate Achilles heel of Iran—and a massive glaring fact that Western powers such as the United States, Israel, and other nations seize on to justify bombing the current government of Iran into oblivion.

On a more sick and hypocritical level, the fact that Gulf states nations such as Saudi Arabia and Bahrain also constantly issue clarion calls for regime change or war with Iran when they themselves host numerous and countless violations of human rights against women, minorities, religious organizations, and *heretics;* still this only underscores the geopolitical reasons that these aggressive nations want to change or destroy the current Iranian regime.

In order to both diffuse and defray these attacks, Iran has no other real choice other than to augment and increase their internal human rights organizations to both monitor as well as organically implement change in their country, subject to the will of their governed people.

By doing so, Iran could effectively accomplish two goals: (1) maintain their current government with relative stability and (2) organically grow and develop to adequately and accurately transform their government into one that faithfully represents the interests and aspirations of its people, rather than appear to subjugate and suppress them.

To be sure, Iran would be giving up some of its internal and external sovereignty by allowing more human rights monitoring agencies to actively police and report on its internal human rights conflicts and complaints, but it would go miles toward placating its enemies, removing their arguments for regime change/outright disastrous war and would also allow for Iran to approach modernity with the rest of the world rather than being trapped in a society/culture which really has nothing in common with the rest of the civilized world anymore.

In a similar vein, if the Iranian regime is truly serious about joining the league of modern nations, then they should not be afraid or closed off with regard to implementing this.

A nation must be confident in itself, its government, and its own culture but should also evolve and reflect global change as it presents itself by and for the will of its people, not repressing them as such.

Iran has apparently had a troubling history with appointing human rights organizations in the past, as is reflected by its handling and treatment of the human rights activists in Iran (also known as HRAI and HRA), which is a nonpolitical, nongovernmental organization composed of advocates who defend human rights in Iran, which was founded in 2006.

This HRAI organization supposedly was set up to keep the Iranian community and the world informed by monitoring human rights violations in the country and disseminating the news about such abuses.

Additionally, HRAI was allegedly enacted to strive to improve the current state of affairs in a peaceful manner and support strict adherence to human rights principles.

However, the Islamic Republic of Iran has apparently moved to both dismantle and arrest many of the organization's leaders and representatives, beginning in 2010.

Specifically, on March 2, 2010, the government of Iran moved to break up HRAI.

During the subsequent reconstruction of the organization, the organization apparently registered as a United States' nonprofit organization and was invited to attend the annual NGO conference sponsored by the United Nations.

While the Iranian government may have a reason to distrust the impetus/ motivations of the United States, Israel, and the Gulf states, it really has no reason to distrust the United Nations, which has historically been its only real honest broker/ally.

Adding insult to injury, the HRAI has also been invited to join the World Movement for Democracy and to participate in the human rights events sponsored by the governments of Canada, the United States, and the European Union.

The Islamic Republic of Iran cannot (and should not) avoid this issue any further.

Merely parroting the mantra that "Saudi Arabia engages in more (or less) human rights abuses" is no longer adequate to stave off and prevent the war drum that is heading Iran's way.

There are simply too many financial, oil and gas, military industrial complex, geopolitical, and human rights reasons and powers fixated on either regime change or outright war with the Islamic Republic of Iran.

If Iran is truly a confident nation that values it past history and desired future, it must drastically increase and augment its human rights organizations (to get on par with the United States, Europe, and Israel) and move forward to finally embrace its place in the sun as its leaders supposedly state that they want.

If not, then it deserves exactly what it is probably going to get, more war, destabilization, destruction, disorientation, and disarray, similar to what happened to Libya, Syria, Iraq, Yemen, and other nations with closed door human rights policies.

CHAPTER 13

After Successfully Reforming U.S. Criminal Justice, President Trump Should Now Reform the Family Court System

Now that the Trump administration has successfully prepared, filed, and achieved historic criminal justice reform—something which his predecessors could not get done or even made worse, such as with Joe Biden and Bill Clinton's cataclysmic Violent Crime Control and Law Enforcement Act of 1994 (VCCLEA) often referred to as the 1994 Crime Bill, which illegally and unconstitutionally jailed or contributed to criminal records to 70 million Americans (more than the population of France), mass incarcerating 1/3 of all blacks, 1/6 of all Latinos, and 1/10 of all whites in the United States—now is the time to also pass a comprehensive all-encompassing family court reform act as well.

The American family court system is world famous for being one of the most cruel, catastrophic, abusive, arbitrary, and destructive forms of court ordered governance that the world has ever seen.

Rooted in such Hitlerian ideas such as "the best interests of the child" and "preventing domestic violence," which seem noble and positive on the surface, unfortunately it is the only court system which removes all constitutional guarantees of individual human and civil rights usually from the father as soon as he steps into the *family court arena*.

The aforementioned Hitlerian concepts immediately subject a disfavored litigant of his/her First, Second, Fourth, Fifth, Sixth, Eighth, and Thirteenth Amendment rights within a closed star-chamber court without cameras or spectators allowed, completely and totally ripe for them to be plundered, abused, harassed, threatened, surveillanced, castigated, attacked, bankrupted, invaded, and destroyed by all of the career members of this family court system—including the various *magistrates*, judges, court officers, law clerks, child-protective service workers, court-appointed attorneys, forensic experts, law guardians, and anyone else who can either make a buck or get even with one of the parties involved in fighting for his/her life or that of their children.

It is no wonder that a great many conspiracy theories have emerged that to deposit someone within the family court system is tantamount to a slow-motion assassination or torture chamber, wherein that targeted individual is slowly, methodically, and painfully destroyed over many years, sometimes decades, subjected over and over to repeated fear, bankruptcy, incarceration, or detention for crimes/transgressions that did not even exist before the family court even got involved.

And it's all done in secret, not open to the general public, for the "best interests of the child" or to "protect people from domestic violence (even false allegations thereon)."

Orders of Protection (OP), depriving people of their life, liberty, property, children, or possessions are handed out like jelly beans because no judge or magistrate of first impression wants to be in the newspaper just in case one of the allegations turns out to be true, but by the time a party is determined to be innocent of the allegations contained within the family offense petition forming the basis of the OP, that person's life has already been irreparably ruined in almost every capacity.

To that end, the family court system must immediately be reformed, if not outright abolished as follows:

(1)   all judges/magistrates must be screened (and then screened again) for any links to extremist, domestic or ideological groups or agents such as militant feminism, leftist organizations, racist organizations, socialist organizations, or any other groups which by nature and definition fly in the face of the United States

Constitution guaranteeing equal due process rights for each and every one of their citizenry;

(2)   no longer should judges or magistrates allow their law clerks or staff to write their judicial opinions—too many times a *life-and-death* judicial opinion governing a family, children, or domestic partnership is written in near *chicken scratch* without any basis in law or fact, merely on emotion, gut instinct, and personal prejudice, by an untrained individual with no background in the law or the constitution, resulting in complete destruction of their targets for arbitrary and capricious reasons;

(3)   Orders of Protection cannot and should not be issued as a matter of right—more emphasis needs to be placed on completely and totally evaluating and gauging the imminent threat and seriousness of both the charges (and the evidence) before these are allowed to be issued, which are also unfortunately registered with the federal government law enforcement agencies as well as with the states and local enforcement agencies;

(4)   more emphasis needs to be placed on family mediation, arbitration, and even counseling services for domestic partners, husbands, and wives to *stay together* for the best interests of the child, if at all feasible and possible, rather than right from the beginning arming both sides to the teeth with legal and equitable weapons of mass destruction designed to mimic a gladiatorial combat, rather than a very sad and sorry state of affairs facing this very vulnerable and disoriented family;

(5)   fathers and mothers must be treated equally under the law and their children need to be considered a part of both in complete and total equality—the sad cultural norm that pervades the family court system that somehow *women and mothers* are always right and are all powerful, with men and fathers having little to no rights whatsoever—needs to be changed and changed immediately as this outright discrimination against men is a direct hit and assault on the very words and meaning of the United States Constitution and undermines the very basis and spirit of the United States of America and what our Founding Fathers and their legacies within the U.S. Armed Forces fought and died for, decade after decade, since the country's inception;

(6)   Court officers need to be trained not only in overall court security, but also in common decency and sensitivity as their characteristic *jack-booted-thug* approach irreparably and for life traumatizes children, families, parents, and their lawyers and litigants in the entire family court process;

(7)   any indication that one parent is actively interfering with the rights of another parent with regard to visitation, custody, relationship with their own children should be duly noted and punished with extreme prejudice. Parental alienation also needs to become a topic covered by child-protective service workers and not ignored or covered up like what is currently the case now in the family court arena. Children are extremely impressionable and sensitive and likely to ingratiate themselves to the parent where they feel most safe, and if one parents is alienating or cutting off the other, then that is grounds to change custody immediately;

(8)   favoritism within the family court system should be identified and eradicated immediately upon discovery. This reflects the sentiments expressed in point 1 above, wherein certain litigants in the family court system are allied with the presiding judge or magistrate on purely political, ideological, sexual, financial, ethnic, or other grounds and then benefit enormously when it comes to case adjudication or decisions handed down from the bench (or from their law clerks, paralegals, forensic experts, or court personnel;

(9)   the federal government and law enforcement must readily step in whenever and wherever these types of problems arise. Currently the position of the federal law enforcement agencies reflect a sentiment that "they do not like to get involved in current court proceedings," but this type of mentality encourages corruption, favoritism, child trafficking, child abuse, and parental alienation, which contributes to crime and other social ills/aberrations and can no longer be tolerated anymore;

(10)   similarly, appellate and federal courts should no longer outright reject appeals for justice from targeted litigants currently wrestling with a corrupt out of control family court star chamber, and it is not fair or moral that corrupt judges, magistrates, law

clerks, and court personnel can claim *sovereign immunity* and thus be insulated from accountability and then be defended by the states' attorney generals and the awesome power and limitless purse of the state when they commit crimes against children and families.

In short, the American family court system, like the criminal justice system, needs to be reformed and reformed now as it is a National Security issue to preserve and protect the integrity, strength, and sanctity of the nuclear family unit.

CHAPTER 14

The Danger of Extremism

Let's face it, we as the human race have to share this world and adjust ourselves accordingly.

Each and every societal group, just like the individuals that make them up, have their own ideals, goals, aspirations, belief systems, morals, values, and opinions.

And we as a human race must learn to listen to one another, make up our own minds, and then try and forge a world in which we can all live and coexist peacefully.

But what happens when one group or ideology has more money, power, political influence, technological superiority, or even military or nuclear weaponry to impose its value systems and beliefs on others?

What happens then if that relatively powerful group or ideology begins to take on or admit extremist ideology perspectives into its folds, thus rendering another group oppressed or stifled without any recourse both legally and equitably?

When this occurs in human society on a global scale, other members of the human race must intervene and intervene quickly.

Various illuminated members of the human race must say something to avoid the trampling over of others who are less powerful, less monetized, less well-off militarily, and relatively voiceless.

Extremism is usually symptomatic of a major imbalance not just in the minds of the individuals making up that faction, but in the group itself.

In the past, extremism has created and caused genocide, slavery, and death.

Human beings of all stripes, hues, and differences must learn to listen to one another, internalize, and respond, not eradicate or destroy.

Eventually, truisms and truths prevail, and if one individual or group has a good idea that benefits all of humankind, then that idea or value system will multiply and spread as it makes sense if it inures to the benefit of the global society.

Likewise, if one ideology results in death, destruction, corruption, or harm, then that idea will usually phase itself out and become extinct.

However, that healthy, normal process of *survival of the fittest* of ideas and ideologies becomes artificially prolonged, twisted, corrupted, or extended if it is backed up by immense amounts of money, lobbying power, technological advances, military strength, and media control.

To that end we as a human race must be eternally vigilant to counsel and defend our fellow members of the human race and both observe and report when we see one group or another being trampled into the earth by another group.

It is the only way that we as the human race will both survive and forge a better tomorrow.

Chapter 15

Unfortunately, When Republicans/ Conservatives Are in Power, Banks, Real Estate, and Insurance Companies Crush the People

There is certainly a correlation by and between when conservatives and Republicans talk about *deregulation* and *freedom* of business in the outright and total crushing of the American people underneath a boot of immorality.

For example, insurance companies will start to increase the use dishonest and unethical *adjustors* to set out to deny lawful proper claims for insurance, such as when someone has fully paid their expensive premiums but then is cruelly and out of hand denied much-needed assistance from these insurance companies for various health problems, automobile accidents, home and renters policy mishaps, professional liability defense, general business liability assistance, property damage, and other types of accidents and mishaps that these insurance companies state that they were designed to protect their customers with.

These insurance companies know fully well that the poor and middle class do not have the ability to hire and retain competent, high-powered lawyers to defend their interests either by entangling with them or in dealing with the entities that are coming after them in the above-named types of life problems.

The Democrats had created and implemented such consumer watchdog agencies such as the Consumer Financial Protection Bureau (CFPB) and the New York Department of Financial Services (DFS), and these agencies were very successful in prosecuting, investigating, and beating back insurance company and banker predatory behavior, but then the lobbying groups for these industries began to buy and pay for Republican whores and populated the congress and senate with their *people*, and lo and behold, we got an avalanche of deregulation from the executive and legislative branches, gutted agencies, and there was replacement of its leaders, all of a sudden leaving the American people at the will and hellish end of the retaliatory insurance and banking industries, and now things are worse than they ever were before.

Similarly, as the insurance industry benefited from screwing over the American people; the banking industry simultaneously have begun again to rape the American people by instituting usurious collections and interest rates sometimes as high as 50–60 percent on such things as student loans in default through no fault of the borrower (due to sickness, injury, loss of employment, bankruptcy), and credit card companies now routinely rape and pillage the American people with ungodly APRs and other *bait-and-switch* mechanisms designed to fleece their customers, enriching themselves while impoverishing their customers.

All the while these banks and insurance companies are charging more than ever for premiums—simple day-to-day processes such as ATM machine usage, finance charges, late fees, and other highway-robbery-type methods to steal from the American people.

The real estate industry, headed up by men such as Ben Carson of HUD, has now mercilessly began to crush tenants and mortgage holders, denying them basic warranties of safety and habitability and skirting all state and federal regulation so as to make a buck.

Freedom as used by republican and conservative leaders was supposed to mean something different than giving trillion-dollar international banks, real estate, and insurance companies the license to rape and pillage the American people, but deregulation is the proverbial *wolf in sheep's clothing* or *Trojan horse* by these communist industries to devastate the American people, and they must be reined in once again by the democrat-led powers in the congress and the senate and perhaps even the judiciary (state and federal).

Chapter 16

Just What Is an American?

The greatest mistake any leader or moneyed, powerful individual or even masses of people (all three of which tend to have the loudest voices) is to culturally appropriate unto themselves, just exactly what it means to be an American based on their own selfish notion of what it means.

The fact remains that the ideal of Americanism is a concept—a truly growing, organic, ever-changing, and ever-expanding idea that is enshrined within its founding documents and laws.

For example, the Declaration of Independence, Bill of Rights, US Constitution, Civil Rights Act, and the Equal Rights Amendment, among scores of other acts of legislation point to an ever-growing and ongoing journey to forge a new nation just like ancient Rome did, united by a common destiny and drawn from different experiences, cultures, cuisines, religions, ethnicities, races, nationalities, and world views.

So when President Trump on July 15, 2019, told four minority female congresswomen in sum and substance to "go back to where they came from" if they "didn't like America," he trampled over their own views, ideals, and experiences as Americans.

Quite simply his statement was an appropriation of what it means to be an American, from the point of view of a male German, Irish, and American senior citizen to a group of Latin, Somalian, Palestinian, or African-American younger females.

Perhaps President Trump should revisit his own people's racial history, wherein the Irish were systematically excluded by the previously arrived and established Anglican Protestants or even with the Germans in America who were actually interred in camps during the periods of World War I and World War II.

The German-American Experience

During World War II, the legal basis for this detention was under Presidential Proclamation 2526 made by President Franklin Delano Roosevelt under the authority of the Alien and Sedition Acts.

With the US's entry into World War I, German nationals were automatically classified as *enemy aliens.*

Two of the four main World War I-era internment camps were located in Hot Springs, North Carolina and Fort Oglethorpe, Georgia.

Attorney General A. Mitchell Palmer wrote that "all aliens interned by the government are regarded as enemies, and their property is treated accordingly."

The Irish-American Experience

In 1836, young Benjamin Disraeli wrote: "The Irish hate our order, our civilization, our enterprising industry, our pure religion. This wild, reckless, indolent, uncertain and superstitious race have no sympathy with the English character. Their ideal of human felicity is an alternation of clannish broils and coarse idolatry. Their history describes an unbroken circle of bigotry and blood."

Nineteenth-century Protestant American *nativist* discrimination against Irish Catholics reached a peak in the mid-1850s when the Know-Nothing Movement tried to oust Catholics from public office.

Much of the opposition came from Irish Protestants, as in the 1831 riots in Philadelphia, Pennsylvania.

After 1860, many Irish sang songs about *NINA signs* reading, "Help wanted—no Irish need apply."

The 1862 song "No Irish Need Apply" was inspired by NINA signs in London.

Alongside No Irish Need Apply signs in the post-World War II years, signs saying "No Irish, No Blacks, No Dogs" or similar anti-Irish sentiment began to appear as well.

CHAPTER 17

*President Trump Has Emerged
as the First Truly Nationalist
but Globalist U.S. President*

What began as a truly nationalistic, jingoist political force in the American elections by and between Donald J. Trump and Hillary Clinton has now tempered into a truly more mature and internationalist-leaning presidency, hammered out and hewn by years-long struggles and realities that President Trump and his administration have had to contend with from both private and public battering rams, as well as foreign and domestic realities and forces.

If one recalls the 2016 presidential elections, the main focus that the incoming Trump administration focused on were almost xenophobic platforms of barring certain ethnicities, religions, or races from remaining in or entering the USA, but that has given way to working with the leaders of other nations such as Mexico, Guatemala, Honduras, and others.

What started out as vague, incongruous statements that "other nations are ripping us off in trade" have given way to targeted and finite sanctions, tariffs, pulling out of various trade deals and working with other nations to either peacefully depose and replace their leadership or outright meeting with various heads of state to hammer out new trade agreements and memorandums of understanding while bashing the unfair or unpredictable actions of the Federal Reserve while dragging the U.S. economy above 27,000 on the Dow as of this writing.

What was once nearly and openly embracing of various white nationalist hate groups has now softened to openly condemning said groups while apologizing for various gaffes speaking of various *shitty little countries* and public renouncing of the *send-them-back* crowd.

Where once Donald Trump rallied against the secret, deep-state forces that wiretapped his person, businesses, campaign, and administration has been revealed by thousands of investigative journalists, public and private investigators, to have been largely true with the public outing, shaming, and discrediting of such heavy-hitter FBI and CIA political operative activists as James Comey, Peter Strzok, Andrew McCabe, Lisa Page, James Clapper and John Brennan.

Where once Trump complained about *activist* judges that couldn't do their jobs fairly because of political affiliation, ethnic heritage, or race has been replaced by moving into the federal judicial ranks of hundreds of new, fresh-faced, and constitutionalist federal judges, who promise to reverse the decades-long corruption, cronyism, and communist-era policies and practices of federal judges that came before, eliminating thirteen rules and regulations for every one that he helps enact.

Where once Trump butted heads with the likes of Theresa May of the United Kingdom, she has now been replaced by Trump's ally Boris Johnson, who, as many have observed, appear to have been his long-lost brother or was separated at birth or was once his friend at private school.

Victory after victory and triumph after triumph have been the hallmark of Donald J. Trumps's presidency, but this has been a long, hard, and arduous slog and learning curve thus far with both the world (and Trump) having been tempered and softened to the point where they can all meet eye to eye while carefully preserving Trump's nationalistic viewpoints to "make America great again" while also recognizing and realizing that Trump also needs to work with the rest of the world to do so.

Where once it seemed that American presidents had to choose between faithfully representing their own country versus working with the rest of the world, Trump has demonstrated that it is actually quite possible to aggressively, forcefully, and sometimes in a politically incorrect fashion bring American peoples' concerns to the frontlines while deftly handling other nations such as China, Russia, Iran, North Korea, Turkey and Israel, Saudi Arabia, and other hot spots into the mix, usually bringing about results that are more in line with U.S. foreign and domestic policy—and this is no mean feat.

Donald Trump deserves a great deal of credit for learning quickly on the job while remaining true and faithful to what he was elected to do in the first place, and his second administration will be even better.

CHAPTER 18

President Donald Trump Cannot Be Impeached over Ukraine/China/ Biden, but Nancy Pelosi and Adam Schiff Can Be Charged Criminally

Pursuant to *United States v. Curtiss-Wright Export Corp.*, 299 U.S. 304 (1936), the U.S. Supreme Court issued an unmistakable clear edict concerning the foreign affairs powers of the president of the United States.

In its majority opinion, the court held that the president as the nation's *sole organ* in international relations is innately vested with significant powers over foreign affairs, far exceeding the powers permitted in domestic matters or accorded to the U.S. Congress.

The court reasoned that these powers are implicit in the president's constitutional role as commander-in-chief and head of the executive branch.

Curtiss-Wright was the first decision to establish that the president's plenary power was *independent* of congressional permission, and consequently it is credited with providing the legal precedent for further expansions of executive power in the foreign sphere.

In a 7–1 decision authored by Justice George Sutherland, the Supreme Court ruled that the U.S. government, through the president, is categorically allowed great foreign affairs powers independent of the U.S. Constitution by declaring that "the powers of the federal government in respect of foreign or external affairs and those in respect of domestic or internal affairs are different, both in respect of their origin and their nature . . . the broad statement that the federal government can exercise no powers except those specifically enumerated in the Constitution, and such implied powers as are necessary and proper to carry into effect the enumerated powers, is categorically true only in respect of our internal affairs."

While the constitution does not explicitly state that all ability to conduct foreign policy is vested in the president, the court concluded that such power is nonetheless given implicitly since the executive of a sovereign nation is, by its very nature, empowered to conduct foreign affairs.

The court found "sufficient warrant for the broad discretion vested in the President to determine whether the enforcement of the statute will have a beneficial effect upon the reestablishment of peace in the affected countries."

In other words, the president was better suited for determining which actions and policies best serve the nation's interests abroad, period.

It is important to bear in mind that we are here dealing not alone with an authority vested in the president by an exertion of legislative power, but with such an authority plus the very delicate, plenary, and exclusive power of the president as the sole organ of the federal government in the field of international relations—a power which does not require as a basis for its exercise an act of congress but which, of course, like every other governmental power, must be exercised in subordination to the applicable provisions of the constitution.

Separation of Powers Doctrine

In other words, neither the U.S. Congress nor the U.S. Senate can say or do very much of anything to prevent or interfere with this power, and if they do, they can in fact be held responsible for violating the Separation of Powers doctrine pursuant to the U.S. Constitution wherein the three branches of government (executive, legislative, and judicial) are kept separate.

This is also known as the system of checks and balances because each branch is given certain powers so as to check and balance the other branches.

Each branch has separate powers, and generally each branch is not allowed to exercise the powers of the other branches.

The legislative branch exercises congressional power, the executive branch exercises executive power, and the judicial branch exercises judicial review.

National Security and Foreign Affairs

The *Curtiss-Wright* case established the broader principle of executive, presidential *supremacy* in national security and foreign affairs, one of the reasons advanced in the 1950s for the near success of the attempt to add the Bricker Amendment to the U.S. Constitution, which would have placed a *check* on said presidential power by congress, but that never passed or became law.

If Speaker of the House Nancy Pelosi and other Democrats really wanted to interfere with or prevent President Donald Trump from engaging in the activity that they are trying to prevent vis-a-vis Ukraine, China, and Joseph Biden's alleged corruption and its effect on national security, they would have to first draft, propose, enact, and pass sweeping legislation, and this could take years and would most probably never pass.

Even so, it could not affect President Donald Trump's actions that already occurred since the U.S. Constitution prohibits ex post facto criminal laws.

Turning This All against Nancy Pelosi and Adam Schiff

To that end if Speaker of the House Nancy Pelosi and Congressman Adam Schiff persist in pushing the said *impeachment proceedings* against President Donald Trump, it is actually they who could find themselves on the wrong side of the law with formal and actual charges of treason, sedition, or *coup d'état* being levied upon them by the U.S. government.

The consequences of that occurring are truly horrific indeed.

CHAPTER 19

The ACLU, United Nations and Other Civil Rights Organizations Have Become Totally Useless

Somehow, somewhere along the way, over the past few decades or so, the American Civil Liberties Union ("ACLU") and the United Nations ("UN"), which really were supposed to be the ultimate bastions of civil liberties, human rights, and their defense thereon, lost their way.

Looking at their trajectory, leadership, and recent history, it appears that they were both co-opted and hijacked by the power structures that be, both domestically and globally, to the point where they cease to have any power, validity, or utility.

Instead of fighting against real racial or religious discrimination in the United States, it appears that the ACLU now devotes the vast majority of its time and money pushing for mainly (white) sexual rights.

And regarding the United Nations, instead of rectifying the global playing field, and punishing xenophobic and racist wars, crimes against humanity, migrant and refugee crises being created in a vicious circular fashion by the elite monied powers that be, from both Europe and the United States, they instead staff their embassies and voting blocs with gluttonous, useless, greedy and corrupted members of their representative countries where they can proceed to line their pockets with wealth at their countrymen's expense, living the "high life" in both the United States and Europe, and otherwise giving sanction and permission for the global oligarchs and their bought and paid for leaders in Europe and the USA to rape, pillage, extort, and suck the wealth and resources out of their countries, displacing and killing billions of people in the process.

It's time for the ACLU and the United Nations to start taking some risks - to start to allocate more power unto themselves based on their own granted charters, and challenge the powers that be in both Europe and the USA in the courts, and in the global playing field using economics, diplomacy, trade and dialogue.